MOMENTS
WITH
MY
MASTER

by Dink Bennett

How wonderful to know that we are not forgotten by our Lord who has designed us to live with Him if we but so choose. How blessed to know that He will not outdate us, nor relegate us to some corner in life, nor neglect us when we need transporting from the care of this world.

Library of Congress Catalog Card No. 75-3949
ISBN: 0-87239-043-8
© 1975 The STANDARD PUBLISHING Company
Cincinnati, Ohio   3037   Printed in U.S.A.

I just want to say
Thank You, Lord,
For legs to walk
   Forgive me my wayward paths.
For eyes to see
   Forgive me my hit-and-miss vision.
For ears to hear
   Forgive me my not listening.
For lips to speak
   Forgive me my unkind words.
For food to eat
   Forgive me my forgetting the hungry.
For promises from Thy Word
   Forgive me my not reaching out.
For strength to meet each moment
   Forgive me my complaining.
For Thy continued love and guidance
   Forgive me my lack of acceptance.
I just want to say,
Thank You, Lord,
For Thy GIVING and Thy FORGIVING.

When I survey God's handiwork, I am so grateful that autumn is . . .

Seeing His world in tones of red, yellow, brown, and green.

Feeling the crispness of the season's first chilling, refreshing winds.

Having the blessings of seasonal changes in nature.

Trusting the Lord to keep me, to sustain me, to teach me the lessons of life in all seasons.

True happiness is found
     not in taking, but in sharing
     not in finding, but in losing
     not in laughing, but in crying
     not in strength, but in weakness
     not in roses, but in thorns.

True happiness is found
  not in getting, but in giving
  not in wealth, but in poverty
  not in knowledge, but in faith
  not in sunshine, but in shadows
  not in living, but in dying.

Ah, Lord, we're a people with problems, aren't we! How often I have been sinking amid the problems of everyday life, going under for the third time, until You threw out the lifeline when I called upon You to help me!

We're a people with problems, Lord:
  intellectual
    emotional
      spiritual
        physical
          mental
            social
                problems in every area of life.

Without You, we'll continue to have "rivers that are uncrossable and mountains that we can't tunnel through."

Unless we remember, "With God all things are possible." Matthew 19:26

Ready for the voyage? Ready for the climb? Yes, Lord, take Thou my hand. Let me be a person with problems, but with THE ANSWER to any perplexity of life.

How like rosebushes we are!

We can be thorns, hurting others by unkind words and evil actions. We can cut deeply with abrasions of gossip or thoughts of malice and hatred.

Like the leaves, we can be followers of Christ, giving His work the proper background for the rose of leadership.

Like the rose, we can give beauty and service by doing His will. Some of us will be buds, young in the faith. Yet others will be full blossoms, shedding glorious effects for the Lord.

Like the vine, we can spread our arms of evangelism and support the message of God's Word.

Oh, yes. The message of the rose reminds us of 1 Corinthians 3:6, where Paul said, "I have planted, Apollos watered; but God gave the increase."

Lord, there are times when Your presence is so
   real to me
And I am very still, storing up the awesome
   preciousness of the moment.
Thank You so very much for the secret of Your
   presence not dependent upon feeling,
For You are near in the highs and lows of each
   day.

Ah, the secret of Your presence is not mine to
   understand, but to claim!

Count my blessings, Lord? Name
    them one by one?
Count my blessings? See what You
    have done?
Yes, Lord, what You have done and
    what You are doing now.
I wish I could thank You enough. I
    just don't know how.
But I know You read my heart, Lord.
    It's written within.
And I know You forgive me as I con-
    tinue to sin.
Help me, Lord, to rid my life of Sa-
    tan's fiery darts,
And show my thanks by living them
    from a worshipful heart.
Forgive me for my lack of dedication
    when weary I become.
Lift me up—guide me on—as this
    race of life I run.
And never let me stoop so low and
    get too busy in things I do,
But help me look upward and kneel
    downward as I depend on You.

"This is the day which the Lord hath made; we will rejoice and be glad in it." (Psalms 118:24)

But, Lord, not today! I can't rejoice and be glad in it today. This rainy weather and dreary sky give rise to that kind of day when I have the blahs.

I look out the window and a blue jay flies by.

I see the various shades of green foliage on the trees and bushes in the yard.

I open the door and hear the birds singing their melodies.

And, lo, the sun peeps from behind the clouds and shines forth on a beautiful rainbow.

And I ask myself: Who can be depressed with a God of love making himself known through the beauty of nature?

Yes, this IS the day which the Lord has made. I WILL rejoice and be glad in it.

Thy will be done . . .

I have repeated those words often, Lord. But I wonder if I pray them more from rote than from commitment! Surely my surrender to Thy will has been limited and many times void.

NOT Thy will be done . . .

As long as I agree with it.
As long as it doesn't interfere with plans.
As long as I can fit it into my schedule.
As long as it's what I want!

BUT Thy will be done . . .

Even when I don't understand it.
Even when it means troubled waters and
    strong winds of controversy.
Even if I must take a stand when I'd rather
    just mind my own business.
Even if I must walk alone when I'd rather
    be with the crowd.

Lord, help me to choose Thy will.

"To everything there is a season . . ."
Ah, Lord, how beautiful is Thy plan
To everything a season.
Thus it is with human life;
For everything a season.

I have rejoiced at Your springtime promises, both the literal and the figurative.

I have basked in Your summer sunshine given from the sun and Thy Son.

I have had harvest when Thy Spirit has sown.

I have known the winter barrenness of heartache and pain.

But thanks be unto God there have
    always been new seasons.
'Tis the promise of a new day
Both here and hereafter with You
That makes sweet the words:
To everything a season!

I had never thought of them as being old folks. Their attitude is like the brightness of a new day greeting the world; yet their wisdom speaks of aging's many truths.

They laugh and love and greet every waking moment as if the very seconds are truly gifts from God. In terms of years, they are four-score and more. Yet, in terms of spirit, they are younger than springtime.

They have taught me that age truly is an attitude. They have showed me that wisdom comes from walking daily with God. Whenever I look upon their faces, I am inspired to love today and wait expectantly for tomorrow.

If we face a seemingly insurmountable problem, why not ask Christ to help carry the load until we grow more in His will by prayer and Bible study.

We need to remember that our loving heavenly Father and His Son will help carry the load for us until we are able to carry it ourselves.

We simply have to ask our Lord to help us and He has promised that He will!

Around and around the potter's wheel turns, and the clay is shaped and molded by the craftsman. Will the finished product be one of quality? It depends upon the potter and the material with which he has to work.

Thus it is with us. Around and around the world turns. We have the opportunity to be shaped and molded by the master craftsman, Jesus Christ. Will the finished product be one of quality? It depends upon the Master and the material with which He has to work.

Around and around . . . let us yield to the touch of the Master's hand. Ah, Lord, help us be pliable vessels, molded by Thee.

I learned a lesson from the landscape during an ice storm. I saw beauty and loveliness covering the earth like a sparkling diamond.

And yet, there was another side of the landscape of beauty. I saw danger and treachery waiting for opportune moments to strike out with unexpected fury and crush tree limbs.

I was reminded of the way Satan works in life—appearing in garments of loveliness, but carrying destruction and hidden danger.

Thank You, Lord, for sunshine and warmth and also for ice and snow with their lessons of life.

Help us learn from both and be grateful to You for landscape lessons when You touch the earth with Your mighty power and unspeakable glory.

Ah, mighty Niagara! I stand in awe at the sight and sound of your power displayed. Men explain how your roaring waterfalls can be harnessed to serve mankind. I listen and accept what they say, but I don't fully understand all that is involved.

Thus it is with You, Lord. I don't understand Your power, but I accept it moment by moment. I word my prayers (sometimes as weighty as the thunderous waterfalls), and I am amazed by Your constancy to hear, to know my needs, to answer accordingly, to give me power, to lift me up, to keep me going, to turn me into a productive person.

Thank You, Lord, for the power we can harness from roaring waters, but thank You most of all for the power we can harness from "tapped" prayer resources.

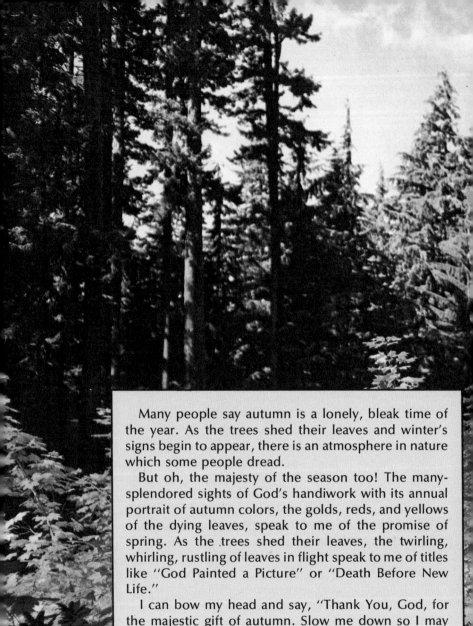

Many people say autumn is a lonely, bleak time of the year. As the trees shed their leaves and winter's signs begin to appear, there is an atmosphere in nature which some people dread.

But oh, the majesty of the season too! The many-splendored sights of God's handiwork with its annual portrait of autumn colors, the golds, reds, and yellows of the dying leaves, speak to me of the promise of spring. As the trees shed their leaves, the twirling, whirling, rustling of leaves in flight speak to me of titles like "God Painted a Picture" or "Death Before New Life."

I can bow my head and say, "Thank You, God, for the majestic gift of autumn. Slow me down so I may breathe in the ecstacy of this glorious season."

I remember these oft-quoted words: "I think that I shall never see, a poem as lovely as a tree." These words express what I feel as I look upon winter's landscape.

Perhaps we do not see the loveliness of the season, because we do not take time to look for its positive portion. We are too busy to take a moment to gaze out upon God's world and all that which He has given us to enjoy.

Dear Friend,

I was discouraged and blue, and you brought me hope with your smile.

I had so much to do that I felt overwhelmed, and you came by and gave me a helping hand.

I was feeling sorry for myself, and you helped me think of others.

You made my way brighter by being you.

Thank you, friend of mine!

Our Lord said He would forgive us
And remember our sins no more.
Ah, if we could but forgive ourselves
And others
And remember our sins no more!
Ah, if we could
But forget the piercing looks,
The words of hurt and anger
Which inflict pain on the ones
With whom we have battled.
Ah, if we could like a child say:
"Oh, that's forgotten.
We've made up."
The love of Christ can enable us
To make up and forgive.

Over and over the drama of the changing seasons reminds me of the change in our world. We have a changing world, but a changeless Creator.

And I need to pray: "Heavenly Father, grant us the love and wisdom to accept change when necessary. And yes, sometimes even to bring it about.

"But, help us to place our faith in You who changeth not throughout the ages. Guide us toward knowing the value of change and choice in personal spiritual growth amid a world of change.

"In His name who changes not, but is the same yesterday, today, and tomorrow. Amen."

Nature's shedding of the old to await the arrival of the new greenery of spring can remind us of Job 14:14: "If a man die, shall he live again?"

God has made His world in such orderly fashion that we can even find part of our answer to life in nature. Yes, if a man dies, he shall live again. Scripture reveals it, Christ exemplified it with His resurrection, and nature reminds us of this promise.

Looking out my window,
I saw seven birds scurrying about in the rain.
They were chirping and
Seemingly oblivious to the downpour.
Like the number of birds,
So also are the number of days in a week.
Each day of the week we hurry about
Filling various roles in life.
We need to take a few minutes of each day
To remember that the Lord
Cares for the sparrow and meets its need,
And He cares for us
And will meet our every need.
Let us, like the seven birds,
Be happy and content in God's loving watchcare.

I saw God today . . .
    In the blooming of the yellow jonquils.
I heard His message today . . .
    In the hymn "Peace! Be Still."
I walked with Him today . . .
    And the humanly impossible became
    divinely possible.

These were silent, fragile moments
When the Lord brought unity out of discord,
    Purposefulness out of hopelessness,
    Inspiration out of frustration,
    Understanding out of quandary,
    Triumph out of defeat,
    Joy out of sorrow.

How sad it is that I often
    Have eyes to see and see not,
    Have ears to hear and hear not.

Lord, help me remember to rely upon You,
    And wait for the silent, fragile moments
    Of Your company!

Oh, God, forgive me when I fail to see
The good in others and more of Thee,
When I use my eyes in wasteful ways,
Neglecting to study Thy Word each day.

Oh, God, forgive me when I listen to words of hate,
Wishing I hadn't, but finding it's often too late.
Oh, God, forgive me when I fail to be
A thankful Christian living only for Thee.